REAL ESTATE MADE SIMPLE

THE COMPANION WORKBOOK

Your Step-by-Step Guide to Building Wealth, One Property at a Time

STEPHANIE WILLIAMS, MBA

Entrepreneur | Strategic Business Consultant | Real Estate Investor and Mentor

B&B
BOOKED & BRANDED
PUBLISHING

COPYRIGHT

Published by Booked and Branded Publishing
www.bookedandbrandedpublishing.com

ISBN: 978-1-969369-28-5

Disclaimer: This workbook is intended for informational purposes only and does not constitute financial, legal, or investment advice. Readers should consult qualified professionals before making real estate decisions.

TABLE OF CONTENTS

TABLE OF CONTENTS

TABLE OF CONTENTS

TABLE OF CONTENTS

TABLE OF CONTENTS

WELCOME

How to Use This Workbook

Welcome! This workbook is designed to be your hands-on guide and accountability partner as you navigate your real estate journey. Each page includes exercises, checklists, and trackers to help you plan, organize, and take confident action.

How to use it:

- Be honest and thoughtful with your answers.
- Keep this workbook handy—refer back often.
- Use the reflection prompts to stay motivated and on track.
- Celebrate your wins, no matter how small.

Your empire starts here!

CHAPTER 1

My Real Estate Goals

Clarity is power. Take a moment to write down your real estate goals. What do you want to achieve in the next year? Five years? Ten years?

Goal Description	Timeline	Why This Matters to Me

Reflection: How will reaching these goals change your life?

CHAPTER 2

Personal Investment Criteria

Knowing what you want helps you stay focused and avoid distractions. Fill in your ideal investment profile.

Property Types (e.g., primary residence, rental, flip)	Yes / No

Knowing what you want helps you stay focused and avoid distractions. Fill in your ideal investment profile.

Preferred Locations (city, neighborhood, school district)	**Notes**
Budget Range	Notes
Risk Tolerance (low, medium, high)	Notes

CHAPTER 3

Financing Snapshot

Track your current financial readiness.

Items	Status/Notes
Current Credit Score	
Pre-Approval Status	
Preferred Loan Types	
Available Down Payment	
Other Financing Options	

CHAPTER 4

Property Search Tracker

Keep all your prospects in one place.

Property Address	Price	Link / Listing Source	Notes / Next Steps

CHAPTER 5

Location Research Worksheet

Evaluate each neighborhood carefully. Location affects appreciation, rental demand, and quality of life.

Factors	Notes / Observations
School Quality	(Use GreatSchools.org or local reports)
Safety	(Crime stats, neighborhood watch, etc.)
Amenities	(Groceries, parks, transit, healthcare, etc.)
Job Market Strength	(Local employment opportunities)
Development Plans	(New infrastructure, commercial projects, etc.)
Rental Demand	(Vacancy rates, popular tenant types)

CHAPTER 6

Budget & Repair Estimate Planner

Plan your finances thoroughly to avoid surprises.

Item	Estimated Cost	Actual Cost	Notes
Purchase Price			
Renovation / Repairs			
Permits / Fees			
Holding Costs (taxes, insurance, utilities)			
Selling Costs (realtor fees, staging, closing)			
Contingency (10-20%)			
Total Estimated Investment			

CHAPTER 7

Contractor Quotes Tracker

Get multiple quotes and compare carefully.

Contractor Name	Contractor Info	Quote Amount	Services Included	Notes / Reliability (reviews, references)

CHAPTER 8

Negotiation Prep Worksheet

Prepare your strategy before making an offer.

Negotiation Point	Seller's Motivation / Notes	Your Strategy / Requests
Price		
Repairs / Credits		
Closing Date		
Included Appliances / Items		
Contingencies		

CHAPTER 9

Due Diligence Checklist

Use this to make sure you don't miss key steps after your offer is accepted.

Task	Completed (Y/N)	Notes
Home Inspection Scheduled		
Appraisal Ordered		
Title Search / Insurance		
Review HOA Rules		
Financing Contingency Approved		
Final Walkthrough Scheduled		

CHAPTER 10

Tenant Screening Tracker

Stay organized and thorough when screening tenants for your rental properties.

Applicant Name	Contact Info	Screening Results (Credit, Background, References)	Lease Signed (Y/N)	Notes

CHAPTER 11

Rental Income & Expense Tracker

Track your monthly rental income and expenses to maintain positive cash flow.

Month	Rent Received	Mortgage Payment	Taxes	Insurance	Maintenance	Other Expenses	Net Income
January							
February							
March							

CHAPTER 12

Flip Project Timeline

Plan your flip project milestones and deadlines.

Task	Start Date	End Date	Status (Not Started / In Progress / Completed)	Notes
Offer Accepted				
Inspection Completed				
Permits Approved				
Renovations Start				
Renovations Completed				
Staging				
Marketing & Listing				
Sale Closing				

CHAPTER 13

Marketing & Staging Planner

Make your property stand out with effective marketing and staging.

Task	Completed (Y/N)	Notes
Professional Photos Scheduled		
Curb Appeal Improvements		Landscaping, painting, etc.
Interior Staging		Furniture, décor, repairs
Listing Created		Online, MLS, social media
Open House Planned		Date and time
Feedback Collected		From agents and visitors

CHAPTER 14

Mindset & Reflection Prompts

Stay focused and motivated with these journaling prompts.

- What excites me most about investing in real estate?
- What challenges am I most concerned about, and how can I prepare?
- How will achieving my real estate goals change my life?
- What habits do I need to develop or improve to succeed?
- Who can I turn to for support and advice?

Write your thoughts below:

CHAPTER 15

Lessons Learned Log

Keep track of your experiences, wins, and challenges to grow your real estate knowledge.

Date	Situation / Project	What Went Well	What Could Improve	Next Steps

CHAPTER 16

Real Estate Team Contacts

Build your trusted team by organizing your key contacts here.

Role	Name	Company / Firm	Contact Info	Notes
Realtor				
Lender				
Contractor				
Attorney				
Property Manager				

CHAPTER 17

Pro Secrets & Tips Summary

Your go-to list for quick access to important tools and websites.

Resource Name	Website / App	Purpose
MLS Listings	[yourlocalMLS.com]	Property search
Zillow	[zillow.com]	Listings & estimates
Realtor.com	[realtor.com]	Listings & market insights
AirDNA	[airdna.co]	Short-term rental analytics
BiggerPockets	[biggerpockets.com]	Investor community & education
TurboTenant	[turbotenant.com]	Tenant screening & rental apps
Thumbtack	[thumbtack.com]	Contractor search & quotes

CHAPTER 18

Quick Access to Insider Tips from the book.

- Always budget 10-20% more on repairs than initial estimates.
- Use multiple sources for contractor quotes; check reviews carefully.
- Screen tenants thoroughly using online tools like Zillow Rental Manager or TurboTenant.
- Verify HOA and local regulations yourself for short-term rentals.
- Maintain detailed records of income, expenses, and repairs.

Cultivate a growth mindset and learn from every deal

CHAPTER 19

Action Plan & Next Steps

Your personalized roadmap for moving forward.

Action Item	Deadline	Status (Not Started / In Progress / Completed)	Notes
Define my real estate goals			
Get pre-approved for financing			
Research neighborhoods			
Schedule property inspections			
Set up tenant screening system			
Create renovation budget			
Contact real estate mentor			

Stay Connected

I'd love to hear from you! Whether you have questions, want to share your success story, or are interested in coaching, let's keep the conversation going.

Website:
www.bookedandbrandedpublishing.com

Email:
hello@bookedandbrandedpublishing.com

Follow Me on Social Media:

Instagram: @step.ya_game_up
LinkedIn: Stephanie Williams, MBA
Facebook: Stephanie Williams

Join our community and get exclusive tips, updates, and inspiration!

Thank You!

Thank you for choosing this workbook as part of your real estate journey. Your commitment to learning, growing, and taking action is inspiring.

Remember, every step you take brings you closer to your goals whether it's your first property or your next big win.

I'm honored to be part of your success story. Keep hustling smart, stay confident, and never stop building your empire.

Here's to your unstoppable journey—where hustle meets strategy.

With gratitude,
Stephanie Williams

WORK WITH ME

Your story has the power to create influence, income, and impact. If you're ready to turn your ideas into a professionally written, branded, and published book — I'd love to help.

At Booked and Branded Publishing, we specialize in:

- Ghostwriting premium books with speed and strategy
- Designing luxury-level workbooks and publishing packages
- Creating customized author branding and marketing assets

Visit
Website: www.bookedandbrandedpublishing.com
Email: hello@bookedandbrandedpublishing.com

to explore packages and book a consultation.

Let's build your legacy together.

Tagline: Where hustle meets strategy.

ABOUT THE AUTHOR

Stephanie Williams, MBA, is a Strategic Business Consultant, entrepreneur, and seasoned real estate investor with over 10 years of experience building wealth through personal homes, rentals, Airbnb properties, and house flips. She combines hands-on investing expertise with corporate leadership skills and an MBA in entrepreneurship, empowering clients to make smart, confident real estate decisions.

Stephanie is also the founder of Booked and Branded Publishing, where she supports entrepreneurs and professionals in sharing their expertise through premium coaching and publishing services.

Her motto — Where hustle meets strategy — reflects her commitment to guiding others to build lasting legacies through smart, strategic action.

Made in the USA
Las Vegas, NV
03 November 2026

57420362R00021